FLOWERS

Library of Congress Number: 84-26227

Library of Congress Cataloging-in-Publication Data

Kirkpatrick, Rena K.
   Flowers.

   (Look at science)
   Includes index.
   Summary: Easy-to-read text and illustrations
describe various kinds of flowers.
   1. Flowers—Juvenile literature. [1. Flowers]
I. Title. II. Series.
QL49.K57   1985   582'.0463   84-26227

ISBN 0-8172-2352-5   hardcover library binding

ISBN 0-8114-6898-4   softcover binding

   4 5 6 7 8 9 10   96 95 94 93

FLOWERS

By Rena K. Kirkpatrick
Science Consultant

Illustrated by Annabel Milne and Peter Stebbing

RSVP
RAINTREE
STECK-VAUGHN
PUBLISHERS
The Steck-Vaughn Company

Austin, Texas

bindweed

willow herb

poppy

ragwort

thistle

harebell

How are flowers different?
Flowers can be pretty or plain. They might be colorful or dull. Some grow wild. Others are planted.

begonias

cinerarias

delphiniums

pansies

How do you plant flowers?
    Some flowers grow from seeds.
    Flower seeds are sold in packages.
    You plant the seeds in early spring.

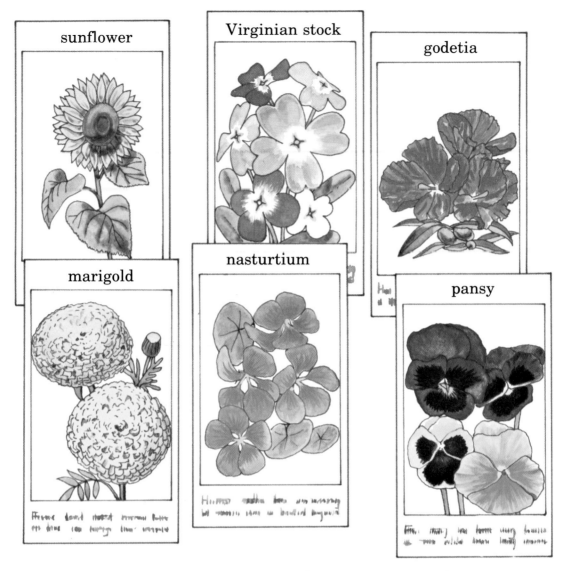

sunflower

Virginian stock

godetia

marigold

nasturtium

pansy

Where can you make flowers grow?
Some people grow flowers in
greenhouses. You can plant them
indoors in pots. Flowers can grow
outdoors in gardens.

Where can you buy flowers?
Flower shops sell flowers. You can
buy flowers that are hard to grow
where you live.

REAL SIZE

¼ **REAL SIZE**

sunflower

speedwell

scarlet
pimpernel

dahlia

Kenilworth
ivy

geranium

peony

How big do flowers grow?
Some grow to be taller than people.
Others are smaller than your
fingernail. Flowers also have
different shapes.

8

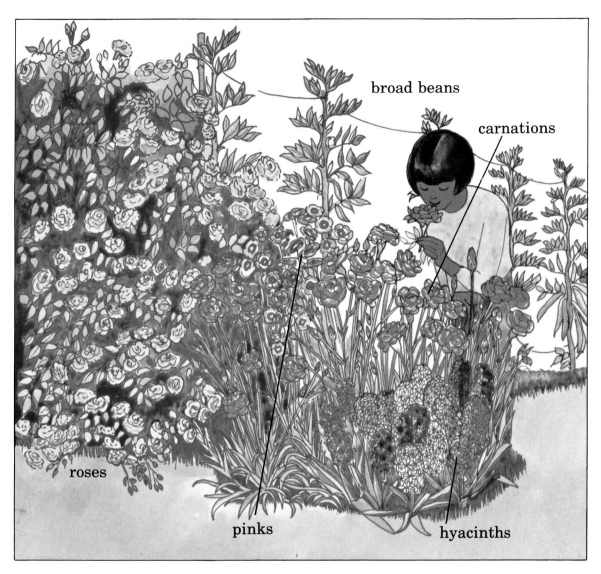

broad beans

carnations

roses

pinks

hyacinths

What do flowers smell like?
Many flowers have a scent. Some
smell good. Others do not.

geranium

scarlet pimpernel

crimson clover

wallflower

great willow herb

salvia

poppy

pink

red campion

rose

Are all red and pink flowers alike?
There is not enough room here for all
of the different red and pink flowers.
Their centers are different. Their
shapes are, too.

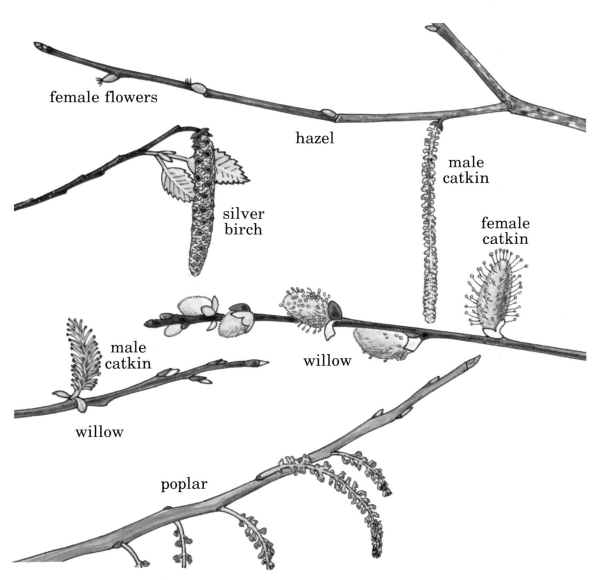

female flowers

hazel

male catkin

silver birch

female catkin

male catkin

willow

willow

poplar

Do flowers grow on trees?
Catkins are flowers that grow on trees and bushes. They grow on trees in spring.

celandine

coltsfoot

Do all plants grow from seeds?
Many plants that have flowers grow
from seeds.

tulip flower

crocus flower

inside a
hyacinth bulb

inside a
crocus corm

tulips

daffodils

crocuses

Some flowers that bloom in spring
grow from bulbs. Other flowers grow
from corms. Bulbs and corms stay in
the ground all winter.

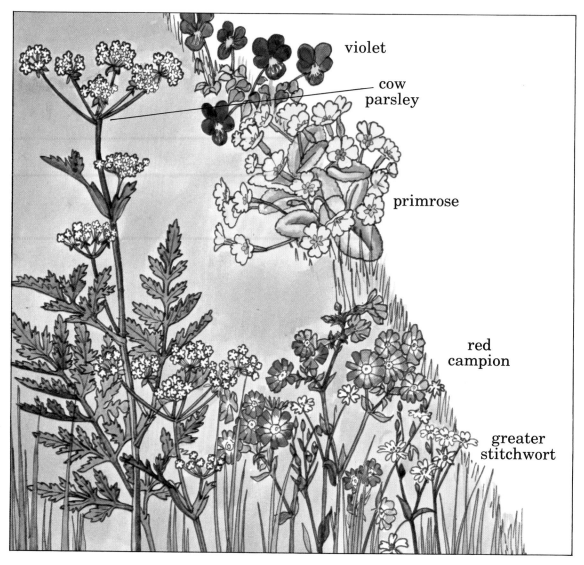

violet

cow parsley

primrose

red campion

greater stitchwort

Where do wildflowers grow?
Some wildflowers grow on the side of the road. They grow in early summer. They need a lot of sunshine.

Other wildflowers grow best in wet places. Some grow well on the banks of streams.

There are flowers that grow best in shady places. They grow well in forests.

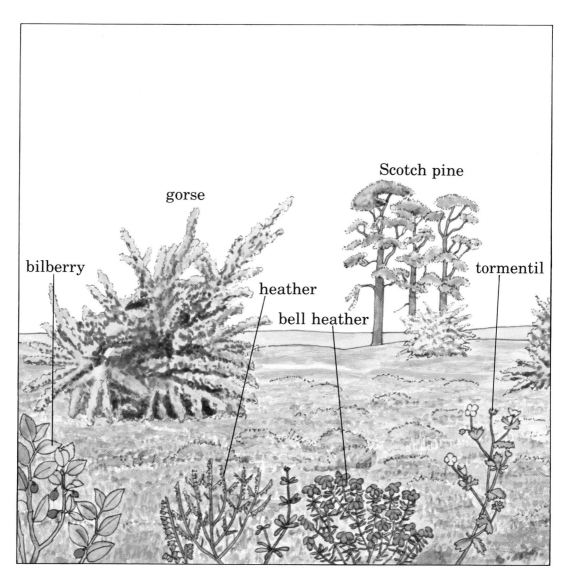

Still other flowers can grow in dry, rough soil. One kind of dry field is called a heath.

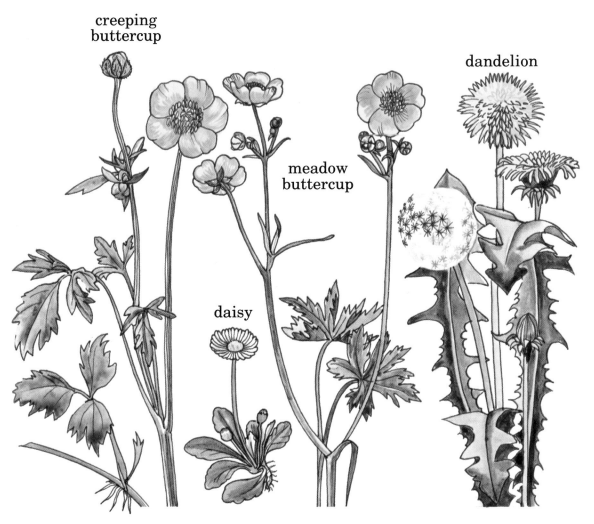

creeping
buttercup

dandelion

meadow
buttercup

daisy

Some flowers grow in all kinds of
places. The dandelion is one of them.
Dandelions have long roots.

inside a buttercup

inside a daisy

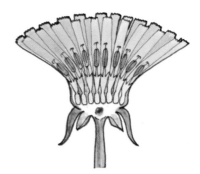

inside a dandelion

What does a flower look like through a magnifying glass?

Flowers have tiny parts. They have tiny hairs on the inside.

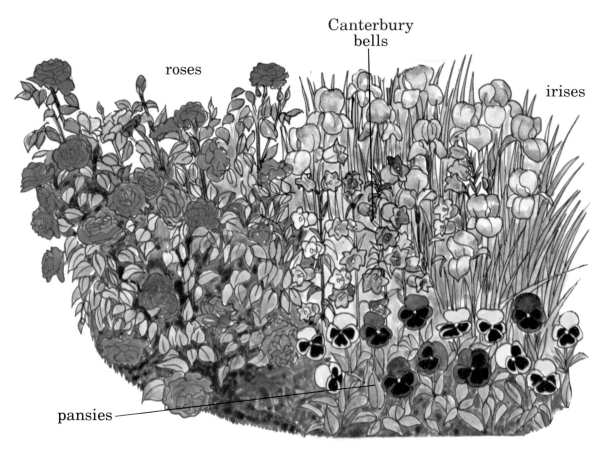

Canterbury
bells

roses

irises

pansies

What are the parts of flower plants?
Flowers grow on plants. Plants also
have stems, leaves, and roots.

sweet peas

snapdragons

lupines

phlox

What are stems like?

Some flowers have very long stems.
They can climb up walls. Other
flowers have very short stems.

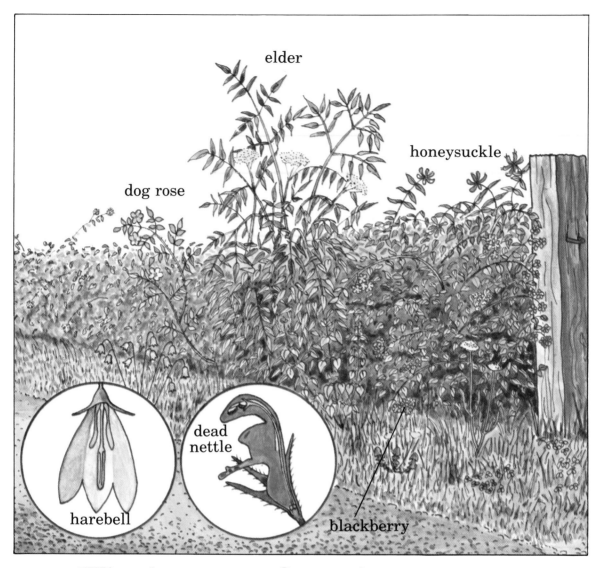

elder

honeysuckle

dog rose

dead
nettle

harebell

blackberry

What happens to flowers?
Some flower blossoms become berries
that you can eat. Always ask an adult
if the berries are safe to eat.

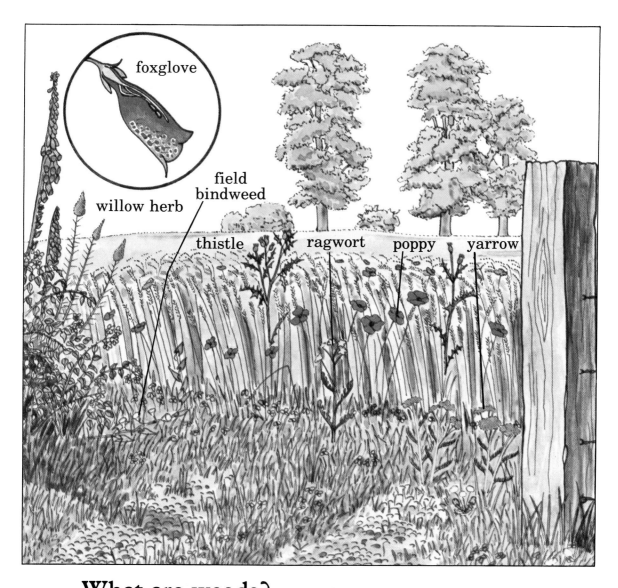

What are weeds?

Weeds are plants that grow where you do not want them to grow. Flowers can be weeds.

bumblebee

pollen
basket

honeybee

red clover

apple blossom

Why do bees visit flowers?

Bees fly from flower to flower. They find nectar to make honey. Nectar is a sweet juice in flowers.

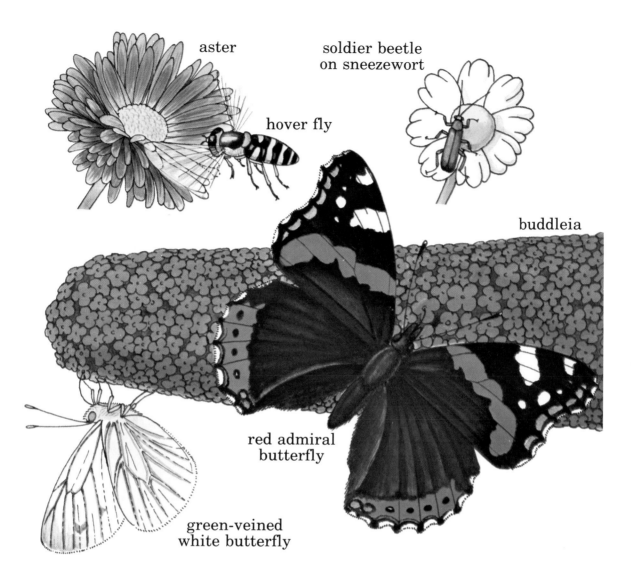

aster

soldier beetle
on sneezewort

hover fly

buddleia

red admiral
butterfly

green-veined
white butterfly

Why do other insects visit flowers?
Other insects also visit flowers to
drink nectar. The bright colors of
flowers attract insects.

Michaelmas daisies

dahlias and
chrysanthemums

Do all flowers bloom in spring?
Some flowers bloom in autumn.
They bloom until it frosts.

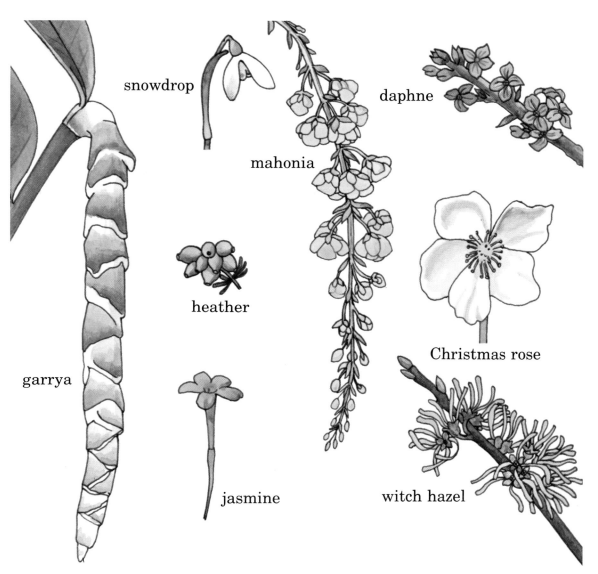

snowdrop

daphne

mahonia

heather

garrya

Christmas rose

jasmine

witch hazel

What kind of flowers bloom in the cold?
Some catkins and other flowers
bloom when it is very cold. Catkins
look different from most flowers.

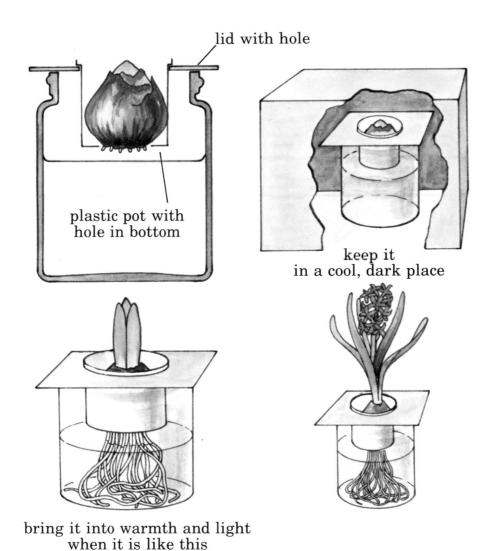

lid with hole

plastic pot with
hole in bottom

keep it
in a cool, dark place

bring it into warmth and light
when it is like this

How can flowers grow without soil?
   They need water to be able to grow.
   If they are started in autumn, they
   will bloom in the new year.

daffodil
bulbs

crocus
corms

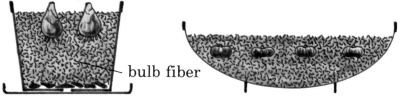

bulb fiber

how deep to plant them

How are crocuses and daffodils grown?
Crocuses and daffodils need soil. You
can plant them indoors in winter.
Then they will grow outdoors in
spring.

Look at Flowers Again

There are many different kinds of flowers.

There are big flowers and small ones.

Flowers have different scents.

Catkins are flowers.

Plants can grow from seeds, bulbs, or corms.

Flowers can grow where it is wet, or sunny, or shady, or dry.

Some flowers can grow anywhere.

Flowers are made up of tiny parts.

Flowers are part of plants.

Plants have stems, leaves, and roots.

Some flower blossoms become berries.

Weeds are plants that grow where they are not wanted.

Bees and other insects visit flowers to find nectar.

Some flowers can grow without being in soil.